DONCASTER BUSES
IN TRANSITION
BEFORE AND AFTER SYPTE

KEITH W. PLATT

AMBERLEY

First published 2018

Amberley Publishing
The Hill, Stroud
Gloucestershire, GL5 4EP

www.amberley-books.com

Copyright © Keith W. Platt, 2018

The right of Keith W. Platt to be identified as
the Author of this work has been asserted in
accordance with the Copyrights, Designs and
Patents Act 1988.

ISBN 978 1 4456 8300 3 (print)
ISBN 978 1 4456 8301 0 (ebook)

British Library Cataloguing in Publication Data.
A catalogue record for this book is available from
the British Library.

Orgination by Amberley Publishing.
Printed in the UK.

Introduction

The period after April 1974 brought about major and irrevocable changes to bus operations in Doncaster and the surrounding communities to the north-east of the town. The Local Government Act of 1972 brought about the re-organisation of local government in England from 1974, creating six metropolitan counties, each responsible for running transport operations in their respective regions through a passenger transport executive. The newly formed South Yorkshire Passenger Transport Executive took control of Doncaster Corporation Transport in April 1974 and brought to an end the seventy-plus years of local council organisation of tramway, trolleybus and motorbus services.

At first the changes were minimal insofar as the appearance of buses in service was concerned; they retained their Doncaster livery with the addition of new fleet numbers until they became due for a repaint or replacement by newly acquired vehicles. The independent companies operating bus services into Doncaster remained unchanged at first, and with their colourful and distinctive liveries, gave welcome relief to the corporate cream and brown that was gradually enveloping the SYPTE fleet. This situation was to change over the following few years, however, as one by one the independent operators were acquired by the PTE, with their fleets of buses being either rapidly withdrawn or repainted.

The photographs in the book illustrate this process of absorption of the bus fleets of Doncaster Corporation Transport, Felix Motors, T. Severn & Sons, Blue Line and Reliance up to 1979 and before deregulation in 1986.

All the photographs in this book are from my original collection, with the exception of those belonging to my brother, J. B. Platt. I would like to thank him for his help with information about various vehicle histories. Thanks also to him and my wife, Andrea, for all the proof-reading duties they have undertaken, which have been a great help to me.

Leyland PD2/1 EDT 703 in Duke Street, Doncaster, March 1972
Doncaster Corporation Transport EDT 703, a 1947 Leyland PD2/1 originally with a Leyland body, was fitted with a second-hand 1955 Roe H34/28R body (which had been converted to a half-cab) from trolleybus 393 in 1963 before being withdrawn in 1973. This bus was saved for preservation and is now at Sandtoft Trolleybus Museum.

AEC Regal III MDT 222 in Spring Gardens, Doncaster, April 1972
22 (MDT 222), an AEC Regal III with a Roe B39F body, had been delivered new to Doncaster Corporation Transport in 1953 along with two similar vehicles. These were transferred to the welfare department in 1968, while 22 soldiered on in stage carriage service until later in 1972. It was placed on permanent loan to the Doncaster Omnibus & Light Railway Society for preservation and is now returning to active retirement after a long and thorough mechanical overhaul.

Leyland Tiger Cub 432 MDT at the Southern Bus Station, Doncaster, April 1972
432 MDT was a Leyland Tiger Cub PSUC1/11 with a Roe forty-five-seat body. It was the first of two similar vehicles purchased by Doncaster Corporation Transport in October 1963 and was numbered 32 in their fleet. In April 1974 it became 1032 in the South Yorkshire PTE fleet. It is seen leaving the Southern bus station in Doncaster.

Daimler CVG6 168 GDT in Duke Street, Doncaster, June 1972
168 GDT, a 1962 Daimler CVG6, received a second-hand 1959 Roe H34/28R body (converted to half-cab) from trolleybus 386 (ex-Southend-on-Sea Corporation BHJ 829). It was to become 1168 in the South Yorkshire PTE fleet but was withdrawn quite quickly and scrapped in June 1976. It is seen here at the Duke Street bus stops.

Leyland Titan PD3/4 194 NDT on an Enthusiasts' Visit to Leeds, March 1973
194 NDT was a Leyland Titan PD3/4 with Roe bodywork. It was one of six similar buses new in 1963 to Doncaster Corporation Transport. In April 1974 it became 1194 in the fleet of South Yorkshire PTE and remained in service until the end of 1975. It was eventually scrapped in early 1977.

171 GDT in Cleveland Street, Doncaster, May 1973
Doncaster Corporation Transport 171 GDT, a Daimler CVG6 that was new in 1962, had received the body from ex-Pontypridd UDC trolleybus 352 (FNY 984), which had been acquired by Doncaster in 1957, and which had been re-bodied in 1958. 171 GDT became 1171 in the South Yorkshire PTE fleet.

Seddon Pennine TDT 622L in Leicester Avenue Depot, March 1974
TDT 622L, seen in Leicester Avenue Depot, was the first of five Seddon Pennine IV236 midibuses ordered. It was numbered 22 in the Doncaster Corporation Transport fleet and was about a year old when seen. All was to change the following month with the formation of South Yorkshire PTE, which absorbed the whole fleet, with TDT 622L becoming 1022. In the background are two 1962 Daimler CVG6s that have received second-hand 1957 Roe H34/28R bodies (converted to half-cab) from trolleybuses.

Leyland Titan PD2/40 389 KDT in Leicester Avenue Depot, April 1974
Doncaster Corporation Transport 189 (389 KDT), a 1963 Leyland Titan PD2/40 that had been bought as a chassis only, was fitted with the Roe-built body that was removed from ex-Mexborough & Swinton trolleybus 394 (EWT 479). It became SYPTE 1189 and is seen in Leicester Avenue Depot in the month of the takeover by South Yorkshire PTE.

Leyland Titan PD3/4 474 NDT in Duke Street, Doncaster, April 1974
474 NDT, which had just become South Yorkshire PTE 1174 when seen, was a 1962 Doncaster
Corporation Transport Leyland Titan PD3/4 with a Roe body. It is seen in Duke Street with
several other members of the ex-Doncaster fleet, including Roe-bodied Leyland Tiger Cub 433
MDT, which is preserved by the Doncaster Omnibus & Light Railway Society at Sandtoft.

Seddon RU MDT 477K in Leicester Avenue Depot, April 1974
MDT 477K was a Seddon RU with a Roe dual-door body. It had been new to Doncaster
Corporation Transport in 1972 and was one of the second batch of Seddon RUs. The first batch
of fourteen, delivered in 1970, had Pennine bodies, but this later batch of eleven were bodied
by Roe. It is seen in Leicester Avenue Depot yard, awaiting numerals to be added to become
South Yorkshire PTE 1077.

Leyland Titan PD2/40 389 KDT on Thorne Road, Doncaster, April 1974
Doncaster Corporation Transport 189 (389 KDT) was a 1963 Leyland Titan PD2/40 that had been bought as a chassis only and was fitted with the Roe-built body removed from former trolleybus 394 (EWT 479). 394 was a 1943 Sunbeam W, which had been purchased second-hand from Mexborough & Swinton in 1955. 389 KDT became SYPTE 1189 and is seen in service in the month of the takeover by South Yorkshire PTE.

Leyland Royal Tiger Cub UDT 455F and Seddon RU CDT 565H at Leicester Avenue Depot, April 1974
Doncaster Corporation Transport in its final form is represented by 1969 Roe-bodied Leyland Royal Tiger Cub UDT 455F and 1970 Seddon-bodied Seddon RU CDT 565H, which are seen inside Leicester Avenue Depot in April 1974. The Leyland has been preserved and is a regular performer at the nearby Sandtoft museum.

Fords XTG 389H and CDT 420H in Leicester Avenue Depot, April 1974
These two Fords were unusual purchases for Doncaster Corporation Transport. To the right
is Willowbrook DP45F-bodied Ford R192 CDT 420H, which became 1020 in the SYPTE
fleet, and to the left is Duple-bodied Ford R226 XTG 389H, which was bought second-hand,
originally belonging to Bebb of Llantwit Fardre, and which was new in 1970. It became 1021 in
the SYPTE. The two Fords are parked inside Leicester Avenue Depot.

Leyland Titan SYPTE 1176 (476 HDT) in Duke Street, Doncaster, August 1974
This former Doncaster Corporation Transport 1962 Leyland Titan PD3/4 Roe, 476 HDT, which
became SYPTE 1176, is seen in Duke Street on the Intake service. It is sporting the experimental
livery and motif that fortunately wasn't to become standard; the only highlight to the drabness
is the wonderful chrome radiator. This bus was one of the few repaints to include the thin black
lining above the lower tan-coloured band. It was later cut down and rebuilt as a breakdown
tender, being re-registered as OWJ 354A and becoming SYPTE M4. It has been preserved in this
condition and still retains its chrome radiator.

Leyland Titan 190 NDT Leaving the Southern Bus Station, Doncaster, August 1974
190 NDT was an ex-Doncaster Corporation Transport 1963 Leyland Titan PD3/4 with a Roe body. Originally numbered 190, it became SYPTE 1190 and is seen leaving the Southern bus station wearing another version of the early experimental SYPTE livery. Note also the Leon Motors double-deck bus in the background.

Daimler CVG6 586 HDT in Duke Street, Doncaster, September 1974
Doncaster Corporation Transport 586 HDT was a 1962 Daimler CVG6 that received a second-hand 1957 Roe H34/28R body (converted to half-cab) from trolleybus 389 (BHJ 899). It was taken into South Yorkshire PTE in April 1974 as 1186 and it is seen in Duke Street while overtaking 477 NDT, a 1962 Leyland Titan PD3/4 with a Roe body that was to have an extended life with SYPTE as a driver training vehicle.

Daimler Fleetline YDT 211G Leaving Doncaster's Northern Bus Station, October 1974
Daimler Fleetline YDT 211G, with a seventy-four-seat dual-doorway Roe body, was one of six such new to Doncaster Corporation Transport in 1969. Numbered 211, it is seen soon after receiving its South Yorkshire PTE livery, but is still awaiting its fleet names and numbers. The location has changed so many times in the intervening years that I struggled to recall the exit to Doncaster's Northern bus station from this angle.

Daimler CVG6 KDT 204D in Duke Street, Doncaster, October 1974
Doncaster Corporation Transport Daimler CVG6 KDT 204D was new in 1966 with a sixty-two-seat Roe body. In 1974 it became South Yorkshire PTE 1204 and was to remain in service until the autumn of 1978, when it was sold on to a dealer for scrapping.

Leyland Royal Tiger Cub FDT 38C in Cleveland Street, Doncaster, March 1975
FDT 38C was a Leyland Royal Tiger Cub RTC1/1 with a Roe dual-door body. It was new to Doncaster Corporation Transport as number 38, becoming South Yorkshire PTE 1038 in April 1974. It is seen having just departed the Southern bus station in Doncaster.

Leyland Titan PD3/4 474 HDT in Duke Street, Doncaster, March 1975
474 NDT was a Leyland Titan PD3/4 with Roe bodywork. It was one of four similar buses new to Doncaster Corporation Transport in 1962. In April 1974 it became 1174 in the South Yorkshire PTE fleet. On withdrawal in 1977, all four vehicles were inspected for further use. 477 HDT became a driver training vehicle while 475 HDT and 476 HDT became breakdown tenders, but this bus was found to be in poor condition and was scrapped. The registration was later used by South Yorkshire PTE on one of their Coachline Leyland Tigers.

Daimler CVG6 198 NDT in Duke Street, Doncaster, March 1975
Daimler CVG6/30 198 NDT was new to Doncaster Corporation Transport with a Roe body
in early 1964, becoming 198 in their fleet. It later became 1198 as part of the South Yorkshire
PTE fleet in 1974. It was withdrawn from service in early 1980 and was scrapped by June of
that year.

Leyland Royal Tiger Cub FDT 39C on North Bridge, Doncaster, April 1975
FDT 39C was a Leyland Royal Tiger Cub RTC1/1 with a Roe dual-door body. It was new
to Doncaster Corporation Transport as number 39, becoming South Yorkshire PTE 1039
in April 1974. This view from the then new multi-storey car park has changed dramatically
over the years; indeed, even the car park has disappeared. North Bridge has been altered to
accommodate the overhead wires of the electrified railway below, while the swimming baths, the
trolleybus depot, the gas holder and Thorpe Marsh Power Station on the horizon have now all
been swept away.

Daimler CRG6LX UDT 404L in Cleveland Street, Doncaster, April 1975
UDT 404L was one of fifteen Daimler CRG6LXs with Roe bodies that had been new to Doncaster Corporation Transport in 1973. Within a year of the takeover by South Yorkshire PTE UDT 404L had been repainted into its new livery and is seen negotiating the roundabout near the now demolished Pentecostal Church.

Daimler CVG6 KDT 204D passing Christ Church, Doncaster, April 1975
KDT 204D, a Daimler CVG6 with a sixty-two-seat Roe body, was new to Doncaster Corporation Transport in 1966. In 1974 it became SYPTE 1204 and in early 1975 received its new South Yorkshire PTE livery. It still had another three years of active life after this photograph was taken.

Daimler CVG6/30 479 HDT in Christ Church Road, Doncaster, April 1975
479 HDT was a Daimler CVG6/30 with Roe bodywork. It was new to Doncaster Corporation Transport in December 1962 as 179, becoming 1179 in the South Yorkshire PTE fleet. Although it received a fleet number, it was to have a short working life with SYPTE, being withdrawn about a year after this shot was taken, and still in its Doncaster livery.

Daimler CRG6LXs UDT 412L and UDT 415L at the Northern Bus Station, Doncaster, July 1975
UDT 412L and UDT 415L were both from the same batch of fifteen Daimler CRG6LXs with Roe bodies that were new in 1973. They were under a year old when they formed part of the new South Yorkshire PTE. They are seen loading at the Northern bus station, Doncaster, bearing their new fleet numbers – 1112 and 1115 respectively – but retaining their almost new Doncaster livery.

Seddon RU MDT 473K on Thorne Road, Doncaster, July 1975
MDT 473K was one of the eleven Seddon RUs with Roe dual-door bodywork that had been purchased new in 1972 by Doncaster Corporation Transport. This was the second batch of Seddon RUs ordered by the Corporation and all became part of the South Yorkshire fleet. The earlier batch with Seddon bodies were withdrawn in 1976, when just six years old, while the Roe-bodied examples were withdrawn by 1980, after eight years' service.

Leyland Tiger Cub 434 MDT Waiting at St James Swimming Baths, Doncaster, July 1975
434 MDT was one of five 1963 Leyland Tiger Cub PSUC1/11s with forty-five-seat Roe bodies. It was numbered 34 in the Doncaster Corporation Transport fleet until it was transferred to the Education Department, exclusively for the use of school children. It became Bus A in a fleet of two such vehicles, which were maintained and operated by the Corporation. It was later re-registered as NWR 421A and still existed in 2015, when it was sold to preservationists as a source of spares for another vehicle.

Daimler CVG6/30 199 NDT in Cleveland Street, Doncaster, August 1975
199 NDT was a Daimler CVG6/30 with Roe bodywork that was new in 1964 to Doncaster
Corporation Transport, being one of a batch of five delivered together. It was repainted soon
after the takeover by South Yorkshire PTE and remained in service until 1980.

Daimler CVG6/30 197 NDT on Thorne Road, Doncaster, August 1975
197 NDT was a Daimler CVG6/30 with Roe bodywork that was new in 1964 to Doncaster
Corporation Transport. It remained in service with South Yorkshire PTE long enough to be
repainted into their livery, but within five years it was scrapped. It is seen on Thorne Road at
the junction with Town Fields Avenue on the Dunscroft service, which was shared with two
independent companies until 1979, when they both succumbed to the inevitable and were taken
by SYPTE.

CDT 569H and UDT 447F Inside Leicester Avenue Depot, February 1976
CDT 569H, a Seddon RU with a Seddon body, was new to Doncaster in 1970 and would be
withdrawn from service with South Yorkshire PTE within weeks of this photograph being taken.
UDT 447F, a Roe-bodied Leyland Royal Tiger Cub of 1969, would outlive the Seddon by four
years, ending its days at Booths of Rotherham in October 1980.

Leyland Royal Tiger Cub UDT 455F Leaves the Northern Bus Station, Doncaster, September 1976
UDT 455F, of 1969, was a rare Leyland Royal Tiger Cub, as they were primarily made for export,
with the exception of the twenty vehicles delivered in two batches to Doncaster Corporation
Transport. The 33-foot dual-door Roe body was fitted with forty-five seats and had fifteen
standee spaces. It is seen leaving the Northern bus station with the Bentley service. This vehicle
has been preserved and is a regular performer at the nearby Sandtoft Trolleybus Museum.

Seddon Pennine XDT 326M Leaves the Southern Bus Station, Doncaster, September 1976
XDT 326M was one of the last two Seddon Pennines delivered to Doncaster Corporation Transport in November 1973. In fact, it was the last bus delivered before the formation of the South Yorkshire PTE. After its withdrawal in 1980 it was purchased by Silver Star, Upper Llandwrog, North Wales, before moving from them to several other operators.

Daimler CVG6 KDT 206D at Leicester Avenue Depot, September 1976
KDT 206D, a Daimler CVG6 with a sixty-two-seat Roe body, was new to Doncaster Corporation Transport in 1966. In 1974 it became South Yorkshire PTE 1206 and was repainted into their livery. In 1980, near the end of its working life, it had become SYPTE's last half-cab bus in passenger service. Rather than being sent to the scrapyard, it was put on permanent loan to the Doncaster Omnibus & Light Railway Society. It is currently on long-term loan to the South Yorkshire Transport Trust at Sheffield.

Leyland Tiger Cub 433 MDT Parked in the Southern Bus Station, Doncaster, September 1976
433 MDT was one of five 1963 Leyland Tiger Cub PSUC1/11s with forty-five-seat Roe bodies operated by Doncaster Corporation Transport, becoming 33 in their fleet in October 1963. It became the last bus in the Doncaster livery of red with a purple band. After withdrawal in November 1979, it was placed on permanent loan to the Doncaster Omnibus & Light Railway Society, who have maintained it in operational condition. It is seen between duties at the Southern bus station in Doncaster.

TDT 622L in the Southern Bus Station, Doncaster, October 1976
TDT 622L was the first of three Seddon Pennine IV236 midibuses purchased in April 1973 by Doncaster Corporation Transport to cover the new West Bessacarr service. All five examples of these vehicles ended their days with South Yorkshire PTE while working the Inner Circle service. They had been sold on by 1980, with some continuing to work for other operators for another decade.

Leyland Titan PD3/4 477 HDT at Christ Church, Doncaster, February 1977
477 HDT was a Leyland Titan PD3/4 with Roe bodywork. It was one of four similar buses new to Doncaster Corporation Transport in 1962. In April 1974 it became 1177 in the South Yorkshire PTE fleet and fairly quickly received a livery change. Just three years on it was looking decidedly 'down at heel' while working the Dunscroft service. A few months later it was withdrawn and converted into a driver training unit – a task it performed for another ten years. That was not the end for this vehicle, however, as it was purchased and exported to the United States, where it is probably still in existence in Ketchikan, Alaska.

Leyland Royal Tiger Cub FDT 45C at Halfway Depot, March 1977
FDT 45C, a Leyland Royal Tiger Cub with a Roe body, was the last of a batch of ten purchased by Doncaster Corporation Transport in September 1965. It became 1045 in the South Yorkshire PTE fleet in 1974 and was one of nine from this batch transferred to the Booth & Fisher depot at Halfway. They remained in service there until withdrawal in the summer of 1981.

Daimler CVG6 KDT 205D Heads Down Princes Street, Doncaster, May 1977
KDT 205D was one of a batch of six Daimler CVG6s with sixty-two-seat Roe bodies new to
Doncaster Corporation Transport in 1966. It had become 1205 in the South Yorkshire PTE fleet
in 1974 and eventually received their livery, but in 1978 it went the way of most of the half-cab
double-deck buses in the SYPTE fleet – to the scrapyard.

Leyland Tiger Cub 431 MDT Departs the Southern Bus Station, Doncaster, May 1977
431 MDT was a Leyland Tiger Cub with a Roe body. One of a batch of five delivered to
Doncaster Corporation Transport in October 1963, it became 1031 in the South Yorkshire fleet
and remained in service until August 1979. The following year it was exported to Malta along
with 432 MDT for the Maltese Government to transport workers building a new dock complex.
In October 2017, 432 MDT was still languishing in a scrapyard there.

Seddon Pennine IV XDT 325M at Leicester Avenue Depot, Doncaster, August 1979
XDT 325M was the other of the last two Seddon Pennines delivered to Doncaster Corporation
Transport in November 1973. It became 1025 in the South Yorkshire PTE fleet in April 1974
and remained in service until March 1983, when it was sold to Isle Coaches of Owston Ferry.
After being operated by a number of Welsh bus companies, it was finally sold for scrap in 1992.

SYPTE M12 (388 KDT) at Leicester Avenue Depot, Doncaster, April 1979
388 KDT was a 1963 Leyland Titan PD2/40 that had been bought by Doncaster Corporation
Transport as a chassis only. It had then been fitted with a 1955-built Roe body, which came from
ex-Mexborough & Swinton trolleybus EWT 480. After being withdrawn from passenger service
in October 1975, it was modified to become a driver training vehicle. One visible modification
was the fitting of an oversized nearside front mudguard, which made this 7-foot 6-inch body 8 feet
wide. It remained in its driver training role until passing to South Yorkshire Transport Limited in
October 1986, and later passed into preservation at the South Yorkshire Transport Museum
in Sheffield.

Leyland Royal Tiger Cub FDT 44C at Halfway Depot, August 1979
FDT 44C was a Leyland Royal Tiger Cub with a Roe body that was new to Doncaster Corporation Transport in September 1965. It was one of nine similar vehicles that South Yorkshire PTE transferred to Booth & Fisher at Halfway – a company which had been taken over by SYPTE in February 1976. 1044 is seen at Halfway Depot.

863 KNU, TCY 662 and FDT 43C Inside the Depot at Halfway, August 1979
Although the Booth & Fisher operations had been taken over by South Yorkshire PTE in February 1976, not many visual changes at Halfway Depot could be detected over three years later. The appearance of a few elderly ex-Doncaster Corporation Transport Leyland Tiger Cubs from the same batch as FDT 43C sporting their new SYPTE livery did give an inkling of the change, but TCY 662, a 1962 AEC Reliance with a Marshall body, and 863 KNU, a 1959 AEC Reliance with a Roe body, maintained the old order.

Leyland Titan PD2/40 389 KDT on Driver Training Duties Near Christ Church, Doncaster, October 1979
389 KDT was a 1963 Leyland Titan PD2/40 that had been bought by Doncaster Corporation Transport as a chassis only. It had then been fitted with the 1955-built Roe body removed from ex-Mexborough & Swinton trolleybus EWT 479. When its service life came to an end in October 1975 it was modified to become a driver training vehicle – a function that would keep it on the road for another decade. It is seen passing Christ Church with a group of trainee drivers and instructors.

Daimler CVG6 KDT 206D in the Southern Bus Station, Doncaster, October 1980
KDT 206D was one of a batch of six Daimler CVG6s with sixty-two-seat Roe bodies that were delivered new to Doncaster Corporation Transport in 1966. In 1974 it became 1206 in the South Yorkshire PTE fleet. By the time this photograph was taken it was in its last year of service and it became SYPTE's last passenger-carrying half-cab bus. It was preserved and at present it resides with the South Yorkshire Transport Trust at Sheffield.

Leyland Royal Tiger Cubs FDT 39C, FDT 36C and FDT 44C, Withdrawn in Sheffield, August 1981
FDT 39C, FDT 36C and FDT 44C were Leyland Royal Tiger Cubs with Roe bodies. They were part of a batch of ten purchased by Doncaster Corporation Transport in September 1965, and these three were transferred to the Booth & Fisher depot at Halfway. They remained in service there until their withdrawal in the summer of 1981. They are seen here at Sheffield, awaiting disposal for scrapping.

Leyland Titan PD2/40 388 KDT and Leyland Titan PD3/4 477 HDT at Leicester Avenue Depot, November 1985
388 KDT was another 1963 Leyland Titan PD2/40 that had been bought as a chassis only. As with others like it, it was fitted with the Roe-built body, this time removed from former trolleybus 395, becoming Doncaster Corporation Transport 189. Also seen is 477 NDT, a Leyland Titan PD3/4 with Roe bodywork. Along with ex-Sheffield City Transport Daimler CRG6LXB HWB 243J, they are seen at Leicester Avenue Depot as part of the driver training fleet. Both the Leylands are still in existence, with 388 KDT being preserved at the South Yorkshire Transport Museum, Sheffield, while 477 HDT was last reported in Ketchikan, Alaska.

Felix Motors Ltd Garter Logo, September 1976
From the mid-1920s, Felix used a representation of the Felix the Cat cartoon character on the sides of their buses. This was discontinued, possibly when Felix became a limited company, and a simple FELIX MOTORS LTD lettered sign was carried instead, sometimes on and sometimes below the waist rail. Felix 34 was the first to carry the garter design and later buses were similarly treated. At least one other company, which continued to use the cat design and the name 'Felix', altered their logo after being contacted by the copyright owners of the cartoon cat. (Photograph J. B. Platt)

AEC Regent V TWR 174 in Thorne, March 1961
Between 1956 and 1958, Felix ordered four new double-deck buses from AEC. TWR 174 was the 1957 purchase, numbered 37 in the fleet, and like 35 and 36 before it, and 39, which came the following year, it was fitted with a Roe body seating thirty-three in the upper saloon and twenty-eight in the lower. 37 is about to turn left on the road from Moorends into Thorne town centre when seen. This junction was and still is known simply as 'The Traffic Lights', because they used to be the only set in Thorne. (Photograph J. B. Platt)

AEC Regent III LWY 942 at Christ Church, Doncaster, July 1963
LWY 942, an AEC Regent III with Roe bodywork, had been purchased new by Felix Motors in 1953. It remained in service with the company until 1966, after which it went to work for A1 Service Ltd, Ardrossan, before being scrapped in 1970.

AEC Reliance EWY 590C in Scarborough, July 1969
AEC Reliance EWY 590C with a Plaxton body was new to Felix Motors in 1965. It is seen in Scarborough on a regular excursion. After the takeover by South Yorkshire PTE in 1976, it became 1014 in their fleet and was repainted in the Travel-line livery the same year. In 1978 it followed other ex-Felix vehicles to the Booth & Fisher depot at Halfway, where it worked for another year. It operated with various owners, including Kiveton Park Fusiliers, until 1988, when it was finally scrapped.

AEC Reliance VWT 355F at Scarborough, September 1970
AEC Reliance VWT 355F with a Plaxton Derwent body was new to Felix Motors
in 1968 as their number 48. It was used on their regular excursions as well as stage
carriage work. In 1976 it became 1015 in South Yorkshire PTE's fleet and was finally
withdrawn in May 1983. It was then used as a café on the A59 near Gisburn, North
Yorkshire, until 1989.

Daimler Fleetline HWW 773J at Christ Church, Doncaster, March 1972
HWW 773J, a Daimler Fleetline CRG6LX with a Roe body, was new to Felix Motors
in 1971 as their fleet number 51. It is seen at Christ Church, Doncaster, ready for
another departure to Moorends. Felix Motors were taken over by South Yorkshire
PTE in April 1976 and HWW 773J became 1325 in their fleet. This vehicle was the
last double-deck bus to retain its Felix livery, but it was eventually repainted into
South Yorkshire PTE colours in late 1977. It remained in service until late 1983.

AEC Regent V RWU 642 at Christ Church, Doncaster, April 1972
Felix Motors 35 (RWU 642) was a 1956 AEC Regent V with a sixty-one-seat Roe body that had been fitted with platform doors in 1963. It heads a line of Felix and Premier vehicles awaiting departure from Christ Church, Doncaster. Behind RWU 642 is Felix Motors 45 (AWR 997B), a 1964 AEC Regent V with a seventy-three-seat Roe body. The difference in length between the two buses is clear.

AEC Regent V KYG 313D Departs Christ Church, Doncaster, September 1972
KYG 313D was a Roe-bodied AEC Regent V that was new in 1966 to Felix Motors, becoming 47 in their fleet. It was the last in what had become the vehicle of choice for the company as all the new double-deck buses after it were full-fronted Daimlers. It is seen at Christ Church, Doncaster, ready for another journey on the familiar route to Thorne and Moorends.

AEC Regent V AWR 997B at Christ Church, Doncaster, June 1973
Felix Motors 45 (AWR 997B) was a Roe-bodied AEC Regent V that was new in 1964.
In April 1976 it became 1165 in the South Yorkshire PTE fleet, but as with all the
Felix AEC Regents, it was withdrawn within a year. It is seen loading passengers for
the Thorne and Moorends service at the Christ Church terminus.

AEC Regent V RWU 642 at the Dunsville Depot, July 1973
RWU 642, a 1956 AEC Regent V with a Roe sixty-one-seat body, became 35 in the
Felix Motors fleet. It had been fitted with platform doors in 1963. A few weeks after
this photograph it was to be sold on for further service and by 1977 had ended its days
on a farm near West Butterwick. The driver in this photograph is the late, renowned
bus enthusiast Mick Fowler, who had arranged a farewell tour for the Doncaster
Omnibus & Light Railway Society.

Daimler CRG6LX HWW 773J at Christ Church, Doncaster, August 1973
HWW 773J, a Daimler CRG6LX with a Roe body, became 1325 in the South Yorkshire PTE
fleet when the company was bought out in April 1976. It remained in service until early 1984,
when it was sold for scrap.

AEC Regent V TWR 174 at Felix Motors Depot, Dunsville, April 1974
Numbered 37 in their fleet, TWR 174 was a 1957 purchase for Felix Motors, and like three
other similar vehicles, it was fitted with a Roe sixty-one-seat body. In 1963 it was fitted with rear
platform doors. In the 1976 takeover by South Yorkshire PTE it was allocated fleet number 1161,
but this was not applied as the bus was immediately withdrawn and scrapped in early 1977.

AEC Regent V TWR 174 at Christ Church, Doncaster, April 1974
TWR 174 was a Roe-bodied AEC Regent V that was new to Felix Motors in 1957. One of four
similar vehicles, it was numbered 37 in their fleet, and like 35 and 36 before it, and 39, which
came the following year, it was later fitted with rear platform doors. It is seen completing the last
few yards of the service from Moorends to Christ Church, Doncaster.

AEC Reliance CWX 484H at the Dunsville Depot, June 1974
CWX 484H, an AEC Reliance with a Plaxton C51F body, was new to Felix Motors in
March 1970, becoming their fleet number 50. On the acquisition of the company by South
Yorkshire PTE in April 1976 it became SYPTE 1016, and by November 1978 it had been
transferred to Booth & Fisher at Halfway. It was finally withdrawn in September 1982.

AEC Regent V 8176 WY at Christ Church Road, Doncaster, April 1975
Looking smart as usual in the early spring sunshine but still wearing its neat radiator cover is Felix Motors 42 (8176 WY), a Roe-bodied AEC Regent V that was new in 1961. It waits on the Armthorpe service at the temporary terminus on Christ Church Road during the resurfacing of the Christ Church area.

AEC Regent V KYG 313D at Christ Church, Doncaster, April 1975
KYG 313D was a Roe-bodied AEC Regent V that was new in 1966 to Felix Motors, becoming 47 in their fleet. It was their last purchase of a half-cab double-decker and the last AEC Regent to join the fleet. It became 1166 in the South Yorkshire PTE fleet, but like the other Regent Vs it was never licensed by SYPTE. They were all withdrawn within a year of the 1976 takeover.

AEC Regent V 932 BWR at Christ Church, Doncaster, April 1975
932 BWR was a Roe-bodied AEC Regent V that was new in 1962 to Felix Motors, becoming 43 in their fleet. In April 1976 it was to become 1164 in the South Yorkshire PTE fleet. A year later, in February 1977, it was to be withdrawn, being scrapped shortly afterwards.

AEC Regent V 932 BWR Leaving Christ Church, Doncaster, May 1975
Another photograph of 932 BWR, a Roe-bodied AEC Regent V that was new in 1962 to Felix Motors as their number 43. It looks in excellent condition as it leaves Christ Church, but within eighteen months it would be sent for scrap. The outstanding art deco Gaumont cinema in the background fared little better, being demolished a few years ago to be replaced by a brick rubble car park.

AEC Regent V TWR 174 Inside the Felix Depot, Dunsville, June 1975
TWR 174 was a 1957 AEC Regent V with a Roe body. It is seen inside the modern, spacious garage at the Felix depot in Dunsville. All vehicles were kept under cover when not in service and were washed and polished regularly to keep the fleet in pristine condition.

AEC Regent V 8176 WY on Thorne Road, Doncaster, July 1975
Another shot of Felix Motors 42 (8176 WY), a Roe-bodied AEC Regent V. The bus became 1163 in the South Yorkshire PTE fleet in April 1976 and remained in service for just over a year before withdrawal. It was later purchased for preservation. In 2012, after thirty-five years of open storage, it was finally taken into the care of the South Yorkshire Transport Museum, Sheffield. Restoration is still to be undertaken, although the vehicle is now under cover for the first time in many years.

Daimler Fleetline JHL 500P at the Dunsville Depot, March 1976
Felix Motors Daimler Fleetline CRG6/30 JHL 500P was new in August 1975 as fleet
number 53. It is seen parked on the drive of the Dunsville Depot. Within a few months
the buses would be relocated to Leicester Avenue Depot and these premises sold off.
In April 1976 the company had been taken over by South Yorkshire PTE and this
bus would become 1327 in their fleet. It was to remain in service until the summer
of 1985, when it was converted into an anti-vandalism publicity vehicle for SYPTE.

AEC Regent Vs 932 BWR and VWY 179 at the Dunsville Depot, March 1976
Felix Motors 43 (932 BWR), a Roe-bodied AEC Regent V that was new in 1962,
and Felix Motors 39 (VWY 179), a 1958 Roe-bodied AEC Regent V, keep each other
company and ponder life under the ownership of South Yorkshire PTE while still in the
familiar surroundings of their Dunsville Depot. VWY 179, which had been fitted with
platform doors in 1963, was the oldest Felix vehicle used by SYPTE, numbered 1162.
Along with the other half-cab AECs from the fleet, its service life with SYPTE would be
short, as they were all withdrawn before the end of 1977.

AEC Regent V 8176 WY Leaves the Dunsville Depot, May 1976
Felix Motors 42 (8176 WY), a Roe-bodied AEC Regent V that was new in 1961. It is seen departing the Felix depot in Dunsville with an enthusiasts' special a few weeks after the takeover of the company by South Yorkshire PTE.

AEC Reliance 9629 WU Pulls Into the Dunsville Depot, 28 August 1976
Felix Motors 41 (9629 WU), an AEC Reliance of 1960 with Roe dual-purpose bodywork. Originally a forty-three-seat vehicle, it was re-seated to DP41F in 1974. Although the company had been taken over by South Yorkshire PTE in April 1976, for a few months little changed and the Dunsville garage was still in use. I think this was the only day it rained in August that year! 9629 WU was subsequently acquired for preservation.

AEC Reliance 9629 WU in the Dunsville Depot, August 1976
9629 WU is seen again a few months after the company had been taken over by South Yorkshire
PTE, and it has yet to receive its 1012 fleet number. It had another four years in service before its
eventual preservation.

Daimler Fleetline JHL 500P at SYPTE Open Day in Leicester Avenue Depot, September 1976
Daimler Fleetline CRG6/30 JHL 500P was new in August 1975 to Felix Motors and when seen
is still in their livery, albeit adorned with advertising posters and the SYPTE fleet number. It was
later repainted in the cream and brown seen on the single-deck vehicle alongside. (Photograph
J. B. Platt)

AEC Regent V 8176 WY in the Leicester Avenue Depot, September 1976
Shortly after the acquisition of Felix Motors by SYPTE in 1976, the vehicles were removed from the Dunsville premises to Leicester Avenue Depot in Doncaster. 8176 WY (Felix 42) is shown here wearing its SYPTE fleet number, 1163, and an advertising poster for toothbrushes. (Photograph J. B. Platt)

Motors Daimler Fleetline YYG 649G Leaving the Southern Bus Station, Doncaster, August 1976
Ex-Felix Motors 49 (YYG 649G) was a Daimler CRG6LX with Roe H44/30D bodywork and was delivered new in May 1969. It was the only new dual-door double-deck bus of any Doncaster independent. It passed into the fleet of SYPTE in April 1976 and was renumbered 1224. It is seen departing the Southern bus station in Doncaster a few months after the takeover.

AEC Regent V 8176 WY at Christ Church, Doncaster, February 1977
In typical SYPTE condition, ex-Felix Motors 42, a Roe-bodied AEC Regent V that was new in August 1961, pulls onto the Armthorpe stand. At least the advertisement for Italian wine isn't visible on this side. South Yorkshire PTE had no long-term plans for any of the Felix AEC Regent Vs and they were all withdrawn within a year. 8176 WY was bought for preservation in September of that year and forty-one years on it still awaits restoration, although at least it has been stored under cover for a couple of years.

Daimler Fleetline SYPTE 1327 (JHL 500P) in Mooorends, February 1977
Daimler Fleetline CRG6/30 JHL 500P was taken into the SYPTE fleet in April 1976. It is seen standing at the Moorends Winning Post terminus of the Moorends–Thorne–Hatfield–Doncaster service. The sign in the top left-hand corner of the photograph is for the Winning Post pub, which was one of two large Darley houses in the village. It has now become a community centre. (Photograph J. B. Platt)

Daimler CRG6LX HWW 773J at Christ Church, Doncaster, March 1977
HWW 773J is seen once again, this time parked at Christ Church, Doncaster, on the stand for Hatfield, Thorne and Moorends.

AEC Regent Vs AWR 997B and 932 BWR at Leicester Avenue Depot, April 1977
These two ex-Felix AEC Regent Vs still show signs of their former glory as they stand together, having been cast aside by their new owners within a year of the South Yorkshire PTE takeover of Felix Motors. Numbered 1164 and 1165, the 1961 and 1964-built buses had been withdrawn in early 1977 without ever being licensed to SYPTE. Both remained at Leicester Avenue for some time before being removed for scrapping in September of that year.

AEC Reliance 9629 WU in Doncaster, May 1977
Felix Motors 41 (9629 WU) is an AEC Reliance of 1960 with Roe dual-purpose bodywork.
Originally a forty-three-seat vehicle, it was re-seated to DP41F in 1974. The company had passed
to South Yorkshire PTE in April 1976 and a year later the vehicle had acquired only a fleet
number, 1012, and a careworn patina, which reflected the new owner's priorities for their fleet.
It is seen picking up passengers on a bus enthusiasts' outing.

A Line of AEC Regent Vs at Leicester Avenue Depot, September 1977
The Doncaster garage of SYPTE at Leicester Avenue in Doncaster held an open day in late
summer 1977. The recently acquired fleet of Felix Motors of Hatfield were on display,
except for a couple of Fleetlines that were actually being used on services. From left to right
are: SYPTE 1165 (AWR 997B, ex-Felix 45 of 1964) and SYPTE 1164 (932 BWR, ex-Felix 43
of 1961). The next is difficult to say for sure but it is most likely TWR 174 (ex-Felix 37 of 1957),
which did not carry its allotted SYPTE fleet number, 1161, and was not operated by its new
owner. (Photograph J. B. Platt)

SYPTE Recovery Tender and Daimler Fleetline HWW 773J in Thorne, October 1977
Throughout the previous thirty years I had never seen a broken-down Felix bus, although
I'm sure it did happen on occasion. They were always in immaculate condition whatever the
weather, but within months of being taken over by SYPTE things were already going downhill.
Seen here, 1325 had expired at the bottom of Kirton Lane in Thorne. The recovery vehicle
had quite an interesting history as it was a Leyland-bodied Leyland PD2/1 that was new to
Doncaster Corporation Transport in 1948 as their fleet number 96. It was re-bodied with an
ex-Mexborough & Swinton trolleybus body from 398 (EWT 515) in 1963.

Daimler CRG6LX YYG 649G at Duke Street, Doncaster, April 1978
YYG 649G was a Daimler CRG6LX with Roe H44/30D bodywork that was delivered new in
May 1969 to Felix Motors as their fleet number 49. It passed into the fleet of South Yorkshire
PTE in April 1976 and was renumbered 1224. It was to remain with SYPTE until July 1981,
being sold for scrap later in that year.

AEC Reliance VWT 355F at Christ Church, Doncaster, February 1979
For a while, AEC Reliance SYPTE 1015 (VWT 355F), which was new to Felix Motors in 1968 as their number 48, was allocated to the Dunscroft garage, formerly the premises of T. Severn & Son Ltd. At that time all the services formerly operated by Felix, Severn, Blue Line and Reliance (except the Armthorpe route) were worked by the Dunscroft garage, and 1015, contrary to its destination display, was about to begin a relief working on the Dunscroft route with driver Michael Fowler in charge. The Goole service had actually departed a few minutes earlier, so this was really a posed picture. (Photograph J. B. Platt)

Daimler CRG6LX SWT 433L at Christ Church, Doncaster, February 1979
SWT 433L was a Roe-bodied Daimler CRG6LX that was new to Felix Motors in September 1972, numbered 52. It was transferred to South Yorkshire PTE in April 1976, becoming SYPTE 1326. It received its new livery in early 1977 and remained with the PTE until August 1984, when it was sold to Leon Motors of Finningley for further service. It became 105 in their fleet and was eventually dismantled for spares in 1990. (Photograph J. B. Platt)

AEC Reliances 493 DWW and CWX 484H at Booth & Fisher Depot, Halfway, May 1979
493 DWW and CWX 484H were both AEC Reliances: 493 DWW had been new to Felix
Motors in June 1963 and had a C43F Duple body, while CWX 484H had been new in March
1970. After the takeover by South Yorkshire PTE they became 1013 and 1016 respectively and
were very soon transferred to operate with the Booth & Fisher fleet. 1013 remained in service
until September 1979, after which it completed a student group expedition from the Arctic to
Spain before being scrapped in 1982. 1016 remained in service until September 1982, before
succumbing to the scrap man in the summer of 1986.

AEC Reliance 9629 WU at Booth & Fisher Depot, Halfway, February 1980
9629 WU, an AEC Reliance of 1960 with Roe dual-purpose bodywork, had completed four
years of service for its new owners, most of which had been from the Booth & Fisher depot at
Halfway. It was purchased for preservation shortly afterwards and now resides at the Trolleybus
Museum, Sandtoft, not far from its original home.

AEC Regent V RWU 643 at Thorn Ultra Newport, Isle of Wight, October 1980
Felix Motors 36 (RWU 643) was a 1956 AEC Regent V with a sixty-one-seat Roe body that had been fitted with platform doors in 1963. It was sold out of service in March 1973 to Thorn Consumer Electronics Limited in Gosport. It was finally scrapped in early 1983, having had a working life of twenty-six years.

Guy Arab IV 7014 YG in Armthorpe, March 1962
7014 YG was the first of a series of Roe-bodied seventy-three-seat Guy double-deckers that joined the fleet from 1962. This one had the Johannesburg-style radiator cover. Roe applied a darker shade of blue than on the previously supplied Burlingham-bodied double-deck buses, but reverted to 'Danube' blue with the next order. 7014 YG is photographed outside Blue Line's garage in Woodlea, Armthorpe. (Photograph J. B. Platt)

Barnaby-bodied Leyland Comet JWX 261 in Moorends, July 1962
Seen in July 1962 at Moorends on a miners' service shortly before withdrawal, JWX 261 was one of two normal control Leyland Comets operated by R. Store Ltd, and was in fact the last vehicle ordered by Mr Store before he sold the business to Blue Line. It was retained in service for a longer period than usual as, being under 5 tons in weight, it was able to operate the Saturdays-only service between Kirkhouse Green and Doncaster via Trumfleet, Braithwaite, Kirk Bramwith and Barnby Dun. This was due to the route including a canal bridge that had a 5-ton limit. (Photograph J. B. Platt)

Guy Arab III HWU 438 in Moorends, July 1962
HWU 438 waits on Marshland Road, close to Grange Road in Moorends, during July 1962 before loading miners for an afternoon shift at Rossington Colliery. The collieries worked three shifts and these services were provided throughout the day and night for miners who had formerly worked at Thorne Colliery, which had closed in 1956 after serious flooding problems. HWU 438, a Guy Arab III with a Park Royal-designed fifty-six-seat body, built and fitted by Guy, was one of a pair delivered new in 1947. It was withdrawn in 1968. (Photograph J. B. Platt)

The Farewell Tour of Guy LUF LJW 336, Finningley, December 1964
Although LJW 336 was designated UF (Underfloor-Engined), it was the prototype
for Guy's LUF (Lightweight Underfloor) type, and was built in 1953. The engine was
a Gardner 6HLW and the forty-four-seat bodywork was by Saunders Roe (Saro).
It spent two years as a demonstrator for Guy Motors before being acquired by Samuel
Morgan Ltd. The original red and cream livery was eventually replaced by the overall
Danube blue livery, as seen here, although it was always known to the crews as 'the
big red 'un'. It was finally retired in December 1964 and is seen on its farewell tour
with the Doncaster Omnibus & Light Railway Society. (Photograph J. B. Platt)

Guy Arab IV TYG 4 in Goole, 22 February 1967
This is Burlingham-bodied Guy Arab IV TYG 4 at North Street in Goole. Following
the phenomenal success of SWU 876, the first Blue Line seventy-three-seater in 1956,
which ran exclusively on the Armthorpe route (initially), TYG 4 was acquired in 1957
to operate the Reliance share of the Doncaster to Dunscroft route. When the Guy Arab
Vs came along, and road-widening had taken place on the Johnny Moor Long Lane
between Moorends and Rawcliffe, TYG 4 was allowed to venture as far as Rawcliffe
Bridge and eventually to Goole when the 5-ton limit on that bridge was removed.
The fish and chip shop behind the bus, so handy for crews on evening journeys to
Goole since they were happy to serve cups of tea as well, had closed permanently by
this time. The whole terrace was awaiting demolition before this area of Goole was
redeveloped, with a supermarket and its car park later occupying the location.

Burlingham-bodied Guy Arab IV TYG 4 in Goole, February 1967
Reliance TYG 4 is seen departing from the North Street terminus on the service to
Doncaster – a distance of around 25 miles. The original Goole terminus had been in
Ouse Street, but that area had been redeveloped as a leisure centre.

Guy Arab II FPT 205 Off the Road at Rawcliffe Bridge, March 1968
On the notoriously narrow Johnny Moor Long Lane between Moorends and Rawcliffe
Bridge there was little room for error. This is actually Moor Road at the Rawcliffe
Bridge end of Johnny Moor Long Lane and the grassy area is the raised bank of the
canalised River Don, known as the Dutch River. The soft, swampy margins of the road
were quite dangerous. In this case, the bus was travelling quite slowly as it moved over
to the left to allow an approaching lorry to pass. Unfortunately, the nearside front
wheel began to sink as it reached the edge of the tarmac, and as the point of no return
was reached, the vehicle tilted. There were several injuries but fortunately no loss of
life as a result of this spectacular accident. (Photograph J. B. Platt)

Fred Cross Leyland Recovery Vehicle RYG 345F Attends Guy Arab II FPT 205, March 1968
Two recovery vehicles were involved in the process, during which the bus swung round almost
90 degrees clockwise as it was raised. It appeared to have suffered relatively little damage and
had only one broken window on the nearside. Nevertheless, it was considered a write-off and
went for scrap. FPT 207 (formerly numbered 178 in the Sunderland & District Omnibus fleet),
which was assigned to Reliance, continued in service until withdrawal later in 1968. (Photograph
J. B. Platt)

Blue Line Guy Arab V RWY 891F at Christ Church, Doncaster, March 1969
Between 1963 and 1967, S. Morgan Ltd and R. Store Ltd took delivery of six Guy Arab V
double-deck buses. They were all fitted with seventy-three-seat front-entrance bodies by Charles
H. Roe of Crossgates, Leeds. RWY 891F is seen at Christ Church on the Armthorpe service with
Felix AEC Regent V VWY 179 in the background.

Guy Arab IV SWU 876 at Christ Church, Doncaster, June 1970
SWU 876 was the first high-capacity (seventy-eight seats) vehicle acquired by Blue Line, indeed the first to be operated by an independent bus company in the area. It was demonstrated at the 1956 Commercial Motor Show in London. By the time of the photograph its Meadows engine had been replaced by a (slightly longer) Gardner 6LW unit, which necessitated a modification to the radiator grille. (Photograph J. B. Platt)

Blue Line DUG 166C, DUG 167C and HWW 763J at Armthorpe, May 1973
Leyland PD3/A/1/Roe H41/32RDs DUG 166C and DUG 167C were new in 1965 to Kippax & District Motor Services and were offered for sale when parent company Wallace Arnold withdrew from the stage carriage business in 1968. The Leylands had rear doors, unlike all of the new double-deck buses acquired by Blue Line since 1959. Nevertheless, they were popular with passengers and crews alike and remained in service at Armthorpe until the company ceased trading. They were retained by SYPTE after the takeover with fleet numbers 1130 and 1131. HWW 763J was one of four Daimler CRG6LXs bought by Blue Line/Reliance in 1971.

Blue Line SWU 876 and LWT 500 at Cauldwells, Stainforth, May 1973
LWT 500, a Guy Arab Mark III with Park Royal-designed bodywork that was assembled by Guy, was new to Blue Line in 1952. After twenty-one years and 750,000 miles it has been cast aside, along with its companions. To the immediate left, SWU 876 had once been the pride of the fleet and had been exhibited at the Commercial Motor Show in London in 1956. It was a Guy Arab IV with a Burlingham body and was the first high-capacity double-deck bus to enter service with any of the Doncaster area independents. Its original Meadows engine had been replaced by a (slightly longer) Gardner 6LW unit, which necessitated a modification to the radiator grille. Imagine these retired vehicles recalling better days and mulling over their fate as they await the scrap man.

Reliance Guy Arab V RWY 892F at Christ Church, Doncaster, August 1975
RWY 892F, a Guy Arab V with Roe bodywork, is seen at the once-familiar Doncaster terminus of Christ Church. On one of the final days of operation from the Reliance garage of R. Store Ltd in Stainforth in March 1979, RWY 892F left the narrow road between Moorends and Rawcliffe and was rendered unserviceable.

Guy Arab V RWY 892F in Christ Church Road, Doncaster, April 1975
RWY 892F, a Guy Arab V with Roe bodywork, had been new to Reliance Motors in August
1967 and was the last new half-cab double-deck bus in the fleet. It remained a one-operator
vehicle because it was written off after an accident on nearly the last day before the takeover by
South Yorkshire PTE. It is seen at a temporary terminus in Christ Church Road while the roads
around Christ Church terminus were being resurfaced.

Leyland PD3 DUG 167C arriving at Christ Church, October 1975
DUG 167C was a three-year-old Leyland PD3/A/1/Roe H41/32RD when purchased by Blue
Line in 1968. It is seen on one of its regular duties – working the Armthorpe to Christ Church
service. Like its sister vehicle, DUG 166C, it was popular with passengers and crews alike and
remained in service at Armthorpe until the company ceased trading.

Guy Arab IV 7014 YG in Stainforth, September 1976
7014 YG, a Guy Arab IV with a Roe seventy-three-seat body, was unique in the fleet insomuch that it had the Johannesburg-style radiator cover. It was new in 1962 and was the first of a number of new Roe-bodied Guy buses to be purchased over the following five years. It is seen parked outside the garage of R. Store Ltd in Church Road, Stainforth. Within eighteen months it would be withdrawn, following accident damage.

Guy Arab V CWW 399B at Christ Church, Doncaster, 31 December 1976
When new in 1964, CWW 399B, a Guy Arab V with Roe bodywork, was usually reserved for use on the Reliance share of the Doncaster to Dunscroft route, but the arrival of further Arab Vs in 1966 and 1967 and a pair of Daimler Fleetlines in 1971 saw it relegated to the somewhat less lucrative Doncaster to Goole route.

Guy Arab IV 7014 YG at Waterdale, Doncaster, January 1977
7014 YG is seen again, this time at Waterdale on a DO&LRS tour. Within a few months it would be withdrawn. (Photograph J. B. Platt)

Daimler Fleetline JKY 263P at Woodlea Depot, Armthorpe, March 1977
JKY 263P was one of a pair of Daimler CRG6LXs with Roe H44/34F bodies acquired new in 1975. It is seen at the Blue Line garage at Woodlea, Armthorpe. The destination blind refers to a regular match-day service that was operated from Thorne and Armthorpe to convey supporters of Doncaster Rovers AFC to the home games.

Guy Arab V NWT 496D at Christ Church, Doncaster, March 1977
The crew of NWT 496D – a Guy Arab V of 1966 manufacture with a Roe body
from the Reliance fleet of R. Store Ltd of Stainforth – enjoy a few moments in the
early spring sunshine before departing on the Doncaster to Kirk Sandall, Barnby Dun,
Stainforth, Thorne, Moorends, Rawcliffe Bridge and Rawcliffe to Goole service. The
25-mile journey was the longest regular service undertaken by any of the independent
operators featured in this book. (Photograph J. B. Platt)

Guy LUF LJW 336 at Cauldwell's, Stainforth, May 1977
For fourteen years after withdrawal in December 1964, LJW 336 was used as an
office, with the passenger seats having been removed and electric light, heating and
a telephone and desk installed. Although this led to the seats deteriorating beyond
repair, having been stored separately in a shed, it was undoubtedly a key factor in
the survival of the vehicle and its eventual availability for restoration. In 1979 the
bus was acquired for preservation and the process of repainting and restoring it to
running order began, all while the bus remained stored at the same location.

Ford R1114 MHL 322P at Christ Church, Doncaster, August 1977
MHL 322P, a Ford R1114 with a fifty-three-seat Duple Dominant Express body, was new to Blue Line (Samuel Morgan Ltd) in June 1976. It became 1040 in the South Yorkshire PTE fleet at the end of March 1979 but was fairly quickly disposed of the following year. It saw further service in Scotland before ending up in Falcarragh, County Donegal, Ireland, where it was re-registered 7546 IH.

Leyland FE30AGR TET 748S at Christ Church, Doncaster, July 1978
TET 748S was one of four Leyland FE30AGRs delivered in late 1977 to the Blue Line and Reliance fleets; all had Roe bodies and identical liveries other than the fleet names. It became 1129 in the SYPTE fleet and retained the same number when transferred to South Yorkshire Transport Ltd in 1986. After withdrawal it saw further service with Dons of Parsonage Downs, Great Dunmow, Essex, and Goodwins of Braintree.

Daimler Fleetline HWW 775J at Woodlea Depot, Armthorpe, August 1978
Blue Line and Reliance purchased four Daimler Fleetline chassis in 1969, but the
volume of new buses in production meant that it was not until early 1971 that they
were completed by Roe's of Leeds and licensed. This also meant that all four became
due for inspection by the MoT traffic commissioners in 1978, which was quite a
headache for a small company with limited maintenance facilities. However, all four
were duly prepared for inspection, including HWW 775J. At this stage the fleet names
had not yet been painted on. (Photograph J. B. Platt)

TET 746S, DUG 167C and DUG 166C at Woodlea Depot, Armthorpe, August 1978
It was in 1968 that Wallace Arnold, in the shape of Kippax & District Motors,
withdrew from the stage carriage business around Leeds. As a result, these two
three-year-old PD3A/1s came onto the second-hand market. They were in remarkably
good condition and were purchased by Mr Wilson even though they did not fit the
usual Guy/Gardner combination. They served the company well until it was taken
over a decade later. Both remained based at Armthorpe, even after the delivery of four
new Leyland FE30AGRs in 1978. (Photograph J. B. Platt)

Leyland Fleetline TET 746S at Woodlea Depot, Armthorpe, August 1978
The four Leyland FE30AGRs delivered in 1978 updated the Blue Line and Reliance fleets. In contrast to the Blue Line policy, Felix tended to use their older AEC Regent Vs on the Armthorpe route, though it must be said that these were kept in immaculate condition. The other operator on the route was the former Doncaster Transport section of South Yorkshire PTE, which eventually acquired the whole service and both operators. TET 746S became 1127 in the SYPTE fleet and saw service with Stott's of Oldham in 1986. (Photograph J. B. Platt)

Guy Arab V 891 GWT on 'The Field' in Stainforth, August 1978
'The Field' was a one-time grassy area of waste ground adjoining the bus garage site at Stainforth. It was at the edge of a housing estate and was presumably owned by the local council. It was rather muddy and uneven but has been slightly improved over the years by the tipping of brick rubble, cinders and crushed stone to extend the parking area for buses. The first Roe-bodied Guy Arab V in the Blue Line and Reliance fleet was 891 GWT, and it also became the last, as it was the only serviceable Guy bus in the fleet at the time of the takeover by South Yorkshire PTE.

Guy Arab V 891 GWT at the Hatfield Terminus of the Dunscroft Route, August 1978
In order to serve new residential developments in the Hatfield and Dunscroft area, the local bus route from Doncaster was diverted along Sheep Dip Lane (on certain journeys) in Dunscroft. Later, the diversion was extended to include Station Road and Crookes Broom Lane; eventually, the service was extended along Station Road to a new terminus close to Hatfield Church, leaving out the Broadway and Ingram Road section altogether. (Photograph J. B. Platt)

Blue Line Daimler JKY 263P at Christ Church, Doncaster, September 1978
In the autumn of 1978, rumours of a possible sell-out to South Yorkshire PTE began to circulate among the Blue Line staff. Felix of Hatfield and a number of other local independent operators had already succumbed, and after the death of founder Richard Wilson's brother, John, there seemed little hope that the business could continue. JKY 263P was one of a pair of Daimler CRG6LXs with Roe H44/34F bodies that were acquired in 1975. It is seen at Christ Church before working to Barnby Dun, with the crew no doubt pondering an uncertain future. (Photograph J. B. Platt)

Bedford YLQ VKW 999S at Woodlea Depot, Armthorpe, October 1978
VKW 999S, a Bedford YLQ with a Duple forty-five-seat body, is seen at Armthorpe when new in 1978. This was the last coach to be added to the Blue Line fleet before the takeover by SYPTE in March 1979. During its tenure with its new owners as 1056 it was repainted three times – first into white and red in March 1981 when in use on council work, then into fleet livery in June 1983, and finally into 'Coachline' livery at the end of 1984. It was to be transferred to South Yorkshire Transport Limited in October 1986.

Guy Arab V RWY 892F at the R. Store Ltd Garage, Stainforth, November 1978
The sun only serves to emphasise how dirty the road conditions could render these buses. On really bad winter days, they occasionally called at the garage while on service to have the lower deck windows hosed down when it became impossible to see out. At this time the remaining colliery contracts were usually worked by Ford or Bedford coaches, but in the previous decade many had required the capacity of double-deckers and ran before the start of normal services, meaning that a bus might be on the road from 4.30 to midnight – plenty of time to get really scruffy. (Photograph J. B. Platt)

Leyland FE30AGR TET 747S at the R. Store Ltd Garage, Stainforth, November 1978
TET 747S was one of the four Leyland FE30AGRs delivered to Blue Line and Reliance in 1977, representing the final manifestation of double-deck buses in these fleets. With Roe seventy-six-seat bodies, they had two fewer seats than the six Daimler Fleetlines, but three more than the surviving three Guy Arab Vs and the two Leyland PD3/2s. (Photograph J. B. Platt)

Bedford VAS5 AWX 161G at the R. Store Ltd Garage, Stainforth, December 1978
AWX 161G was a Bedford VAS5 with a Duple body that was new to Blue Line in 1969. It became SYPTE 1057 with the takeover of Blue Line and Reliance in March 1979, before being sold to T. Wilson of Failsworth in June 1980. By 1982 it was with the Weavers Sea Angling Club of Rochdale, later becoming a motorcycle transporter and then eventually a mobile home in 1985. (Photograph J. B. Platt)

Ford R1114 HKU 795N at the R. Store Ltd Garage, Stainforth, December 1978
HKU 795N was a Duple-bodied Ford R1114 that was new to Reliance in May 1975. Within a
few months of the photograph being taken, in March 1979 it would be taken into the SYPTE
fleet and re-numbered 1090. It was sold to a dealer in the summer of 1980 and was then sold on
to George Wimpey, contractors, who exported it to the Falkland Islands by 1988. (Photograph
J. B. Platt)

Ford R1114 MHL 322P in Stainforth, December 1978
MHL 322P, a Duple-bodied Ford R1114 of 1976, is seen in Emerson Avenue, which was the
terminus of Blue Line and Reliance's Stainforth to Goole service, also serving Thorne, Moorends
and Rawcliffe. In the background are the premises of R. Store Ltd in Church Road, Stainforth,
where Reliance Daimler Fleetline JKY 264P is seen parked. (Photograph J. B. Platt)

Leyland PD3/A/1 DUG 166C at Woodlea Depot, Armthorpe, December 1978
DUG 166C, a Leyland PD3/A/1/Roe H41/32RD, was new in 1965 to Kippax & District Motor
Services and purchased by Blue Line in 1968. It had already been with the company for ten years
when photographed in heavy snow in December 1978. It was to become 1130 in the South
Yorkshire PTE fleet and was eventually transferred to South Yorkshire Transport Ltd in October
1986 as a driver training vehicle. (Photograph J. B. Platt)

Guy Arab V 891 GWT in Moorends, February 1979
891 GWT was the last operational Roe-bodied Guy Arab V in the fleet of Blue Line and Reliance
at the time of the takeover by South Yorkshire PTE. It is seen a few weeks before that event in
very familiar surroundings in Moorends, about halfway through its journey between Doncaster
and Goole. Its new owners would not require its services and it was to be scrapped before the
end of the year. (Photograph J. B. Platt)

Ford R1014 MHL 45P at the Winning Post, Moorends, February 1979
MHL 45P, a Duple Dominant-bodied Ford R1014, would become South Yorkshire PTE 1035 in March 1979. Towards the end of the Blue Line era the Ford and Bedford coaches were used extensively on the Goole to Stainforth and Goole to Doncaster services. Here, MHL 45P is seen loading passengers at the Winning Post in Moorends, heading in the Doncaster direction despite the destination display. In the distance the Thorne Moor level crossing is seen, complete with its signal box. (Photograph J. B. Platt)

Guy Arab Vs RWY 892F and KYG 299D at the F. Cross Garage, Hatfield, March 1979
During the final days of operation from the Reliance garage of R. Store Ltd in Stainforth in March 1979, both Reliance RWY 892F and Blue Line KYG 299D left the narrow road between Moorends and Rawcliffe and were rendered unserviceable. The road to Rawcliffe was very narrow, with soft grass verges on either side. If the front wheel left the tarmac, it was very difficult to regain the road again as the verge simply gave way under the weight of the vehicle. The first vehicle left the road on the way from Goole and fell onto its side. The second came off the road later in the day, just beyond the first accident.

Guy Arab V KYG 299D at the F. Cross Garage, Hatfield, March 1979
Reliance RWY 892F and Blue Line KYG 299D are seen after recovery by Fred Cross of Hatfield.
The result of the incident brought about the immediate withdrawal of both vehicles.

Daimler Fleetline HWU 776J at Christ Church, Doncaster, April 1979
HWW 776J was one of four Daimler CRG6LXs bought by Blue Line and Reliance and licensed
in March 1971. It had been in the fleet of South Yorkshire PTE for three days at the time of
this photograph, but had not received its 1123 fleet number. It was to remain in service until
January 1983 and was sold for scrap in May of that year. In the background, sister vehicle
HWW 775J brings in the service from Armthorpe.

Leyland Fleetline TET 746S at Christ Church, Doncaster, May 1979
The four Leyland FE30AGRs delivered to Blue Line and Reliance in 1977 became the last new double-deck buses delivered before the takeover by South Yorkshire PTE. Already a month into its new ownership, TET 746S looks as if nothing has happened, as it has yet to receive its 1127 fleet number or a new livery. It was to remain in service and was eventually transferred to South Yorkshire Transport Limited as a withdrawn vehicle in October 1986. Soon after it was put back into service by Stotts of Lees, Oldham, and was finally scrapped in 2000.

Leyland FE30AGR TET 747S at Christ Church, Doncaster, October 1979
TET 747S was a Leyland Fleetline with a Roe body. It had been new in December 1977 and became 1128 in the South Yorkshire PTE fleet. In October 1986 it was transferred to South Yorkshire Transport Limited, retaining its fleet number. TET 747S was to join TET 746S for further service with Stott's of Lees in Oldham. When finally scrapped in 2002, its engine was used to power its preserved sister, TET 745S.

Leyland FE30AGR TET 748S at Severn's Dunscroft Depot, November 1979
On the same day that the sale of S. Morgan Ltd and R. Store Ltd was announced, the news came that SYPTE had also reached an agreement with T. Severn & Son Ltd and would acquire their premises in Dunscroft. This was a larger and more modern facility and from April of 1979 the Reliance fleet and part of the Blue Line fleet were stabled there. The Armthorpe Blue Line garage was also closed, and that part of the fleet moved to Leicester Avenue in Doncaster. (Photograph J. B. Platt)

Daimler Fleetline HWW 764J at Severn's Dunscroft Depot, November 1979
HWW 764J was one of four Daimler CRG6LXs bought by Blue Line/Reliance in 1969, but it was not licensed until 1971. The chassis were stored at Stainforth and Armthorpe until Roe's of Leeds were able to accept them for bodybuilding. All were repainted and recertified in 1978 by Blue Line, but then received the South Yorkshire PTE colours in 1979. Alongside is Severn's last remaining half-cab coach, BWW 654B. (Photograph J. B. Platt)

Daimler Fleetline JKY 264P at Severn's Dunscroft Depot, November 1979
JKY 264P was new in 1975 and was barely four years old at the time of this photograph.
The paintwork deteriorated rapidly and bare rivets and cover strips are evident. This vehicle
was based at Stainforth from new and did not enjoy the same care that was lavished on the
Armthorpe vehicles. This is not to suggest that they were not mechanically well maintained,
but aesthetic details certainly did not figure in the Stainforth maintenance regime. However, the
process of repainting the Morgan and Store vehicles into the less-pleasing SYPTE colours had
already begun. (Photograph J. B. Platt)

Leyland FE30AGR TET 748S at Christ Church, Doncaster, June 1980
TET 748S, a Leyland Fleetline with a Roe body, had been new in December 1977 and became
1129 in the South Yorkshire PTE fleet. In October 1986 it was transferred to South Yorkshire
Transport Limited, retaining its fleet number.

Guy LUF LJW 336 at the Premier Garage in East Lane, Stainforth, July 1980
The project to rescue LJW 336 for preservation was undertaken by J. B. Platt. Although the bus
is no longer owned or kept locally, it became part of an impressive collection at the Aston Manor
Motor Museum in Birmingham. It has now been moved to the Aldridge site of the AMRTM and
looks resplendent, having undergone a repaint and had the Blue Line insignia added to its side.
(Photograph J. B. Platt)

Leyland PD3/A/1s DUG 166C and DUG 167C at Severn's Dunscroft Depot, December 1980
Leyland PD3/A/1/Roe H41/32RDs DUG 166C and DUG 167C were new in 1965 to Kippax &
District Motor Services and were later purchased by Blue Line in 1968. They were retained by
South Yorkshire PTE after the takeover, being given fleet numbers 1130 and 1131. They were
eventually transferred to the fleet of South Yorkshire Transport Limited, 1130 becoming a driver
training unit and 1131 a tow wagon.

Daimler CRG6LX HWW 775J at Christ Church, Doncaster, March 1981
HWW 775J was a Roe-bodied Daimler CRG6LX that was new to Reliance R. Store Ltd in March 1971. It became South Yorkshire PTE 1122 in April 1979 and received its new livery later that year. It remained in service until July 1983, after which it was scrapped.

Reliance Ford R1114 YET 178T at the Leicester Avenue Depot, February 1982
YET 178T, a Ford R1114 with a Duple body, was new to Reliance in 1978. It was the last vehicle to be delivered for the Reliance fleet before the SYPTE takeover, after which it became 1027. After withdrawal in 1983 it continued in service with a number of operators in the South East before finally being scrapped in 1990.

Leyland FE30AGR TET 747S at Christ Church, Doncaster, September 1982
TET 747S was a Leyland Fleetline with a Roe body. It had been new in December 1977 and
became 1128 in the South Yorkshire PTE fleet. In October 1986 it was transferred to South
Yorkshire Transport Limited, retaining its fleet number. TET 747S was to join TET 746S for
further service with Stott's of Lees, Oldham.

Leyland PD3/A/1 DUG 166C in Sheffield, August 1985
DUG 166C was a Leyland PD3/A/1 with a Roe H41/32RD body. It had been new to Kippax &
District in 1965 and was owned by Blue Line from 1968. At the takeover by South Yorkshire PTE it
became fleet number 1130 and remained in service until June 1981. It was retained as a driver training
vehicle and was eventually transferred to South Yorkshire Transport Limited in October 1986.

Roe-bodied Leyland PD3/4 517 WY in Moorends, July 1962
517 WY, a Roe-bodied Leyland PD3/4, was just a year old when photographed at the Moorends
Winning Post terminus in July 1962. T. Severn & Sons was one of three Stainforth-based
operators who shared the service between Thorne Moorends and Doncaster via Hatfield. The
others were Felix Motors and Premier Motors. Severn moved from Stainforth to Dunscroft
and Felix relocated to Dunsville, although their vehicles always bore the address 'Park Lane,
Hatfield'. (Photograph J. B. Platt)

Leyland PD3/5 UWU 515 at Christ Church, Doncaster, June 1966
UWU 515 was a Leyland PD3/5 with a Roe body that was new to T. Severn & Sons in 1958. It had been modified the year before the photograph was taken with rear platform doors. It is seen having a few quiet moments at Christ Church before its next run to Moorends. It was to be sold by Severn's in 1974 and continued in service with G. & G. Coaches of Leamington Spa for a number of years.

Leyland Atlantean GWX 553C at Severn's Dunscroft Depot, November 1966
GWX 553C was a Roe-bodied Leyland PDR1/2T that was new to Severn & Sons in August 1965. It was taken into the South Yorkshire PTE fleet as 1155 when the company was sold in March 1979. It would remain in service until January 1981 and was finally scrapped the following year. As can be seen in the background, Severn's also had a fleet of heavy goods vehicles, which were primarily used for the transport of coal from local collieries.

Severn's Leyland PD3/4 518 WY at Christ Church, Doncaster, March 1968
518 WY was a 1961 Leyland PD3/4 with Roe bodywork that was new to T. Severn &
Sons. It is seen at Christ Church, Doncaster, on a Moorends service. On the Goole
stand is Blue Line's Guy Arab IV WWX 671, which is being overtaken by Felix Motors
34 (OWX 283), an AEC Regent III in its last year of service with the company. This is
a classic shot of the location, showing the colourful and rich variety of vehicles in use
by the independent operators at the time. Ten years on, all would have disappeared.

Leyland Titan PD3/4 819C WW at Christ Church, Doncaster, July 1969
819C WW was a Roe-bodied Leyland Titan PD3/4 that had been new to Severn's in
November 1963. After the South Yorkshire PTE takeover in March 1979 it became
1157 in their fleet. By October of that year it had been withdrawn from service to have
its body modified and was converted into a recovery vehicle. It was re-registered OWJ
782A and allotted the fleet number M16. In this form it was transferred into the fleet
of South Yorkshire Transport Limited in October 1986. It was finally retired from
Rotherham Depot in March 2017 and is preserved by South Yorkshire Transport Trust.

Leyland PD3/4 517 WY at Christ Church, Doncaster, August 1970
517 WY was a Leyland PD3/4 with Roe bodywork new to T. Severn & Sons in November 1961. It was to remain in service with the company until October 1977 and was scrapped in April 1978, a year before the take-over by South Yorkshire PTE. Severn's were the only independent company of those covered in the book to use advertisements on their double-deck buses. The one displayed on 517 WY would be totally unacceptable forty years on.

517 WY and KWW 513 at Severn's Dunscroft Depot, October 1971
517 WY was the first of two identical Leyland PD3/4s with Roe bodywork new to T. Severn & Sons in 1961. KWW 513, seen in the background, was a Leyland PD2/10 with a Roe fifty-six-seat body, which had been new to the company in 1951. Although looking in reasonable condition, it had been out of service for six months and would spend more time in this position before removal for scrapping by a local dealer.

Leyland PD3/5 UWU 516 at Severn's Dunscroft Depot, May 1973
UWU 515 was a Leyland PD3/5 with a Roe body that had been new to T. Severn & Sons in 1958. The rear open platform had been replaced by platform doors in 1965 and in early 1975 it had been sold on to R. B. Steele for service with Ayrshire Bus Owners (A1 Service) Limited, Ardrossan. It later found use as a store at their depot.

Leyland Atlantean SWR 4L at Christ Church, Doncaster, April 1974
SWR 4L was a Leyland Atlantean with a Roe body that was new to T. Severn & Sons in November 1972. In April 1979 it became 1151 in the South Yorkshire PTE fleet and was repainted into their livery. After withdrawal from service in April 1985 it passed to the Chesterfield Area Play Bus Association, but by 1989 it was noted as out of use in Chesterfield.

XWU 890G Heads Into Christ Church, Doncaster, April 1974
XWU 890G was a Leyland Atlantean PDR1/1 with a Roe H75F body that was new in 1969. Its flat one-piece windscreen and Albion front badge made it quite distinctive among the double-deck buses of other independent operators in Doncaster.

Leyland PD3/4 518 WY at Christ Church, Doncaster, June 1974
518 WY was the second Leyland PD3/4 with Roe bodywork that was new to T. Severn & Sons in 1961. It arrives at Christ Church, Doncaster, with a service from Thorne and Moorends. Felix Motors 47 (KYG 313D), the last new AEC Regent V to enter the company's fleet, awaits departure on the service in the opposite direction.

Leyland Atlantean SWR 4L at Christ Church, Doncaster, April 1975
SWR 4L, a Leyland AN68/1R with a Roe body, was the second of the two identical vehicles that were new to T. Severn & Sons in November 1972. After the takeover of the company by South Yorkshire PTE in March 1979, it became 1151 in their fleet. It continued in service until April 1985 and was later converted for use as a play bus.

Leyland PD3/4 518 WY at Severn's Dunscroft Depot, June 1975
518 WY was the second of two 1961 Roe-bodied Leyland PD3/4. It is seen over the pits at Severn's Bootham Lane Depot alongside its sister vehicle. It had been withdrawn by Severn's at the time of the takeover by South Yorkshire PTE in March 1979, but was converted for use as a recovery vehicle.

Leyland AN68/1R HUG 33N at Severn's Dunscroft Depot, July 1975
HUG 33N was a Leyland Atlantean with a Roe H43/29F body. It was new to T. Severn & Sons in February 1975 and so was just a few months old when seen here at their Dunscroft Depot. It would become 1138 in the South Yorkshire PTE fleet in April 1979 and was repainted fairly quickly afterwards. Like sister vehicle HUG 32N, it was taken out of service and scrapped in 1987.

Leyland PD3/4 517 WY at Christ Church, Doncaster, August 1975
517 WY was a 1961 Leyland PD3/4 with Roe bodywork that was new to T. Severn & Sons. It is seen waiting at Christ Church on a Moorends service, at the head of a line of five of Severn's vehicles. This was quite an unusual occurrence as three other independents as well as Doncaster Corporation used these stands.

Leyland PDR1A/1 GYG 711J at Christ Church, Doncaster, August 1975
GYG 711J was a 1971 Leyland Atlantean with an Alexander H44/31F body. It is also seen at Christ Church at the head of a line of Severn's vehicles. The coach behind was the recently delivered HUG 32N and the rear vehicle was XWU 890G. The variety of body manufacturers and different styles of body was a particular feature of the company's new vehicles.

Severn's Leyland Atlantean, XWU 890G, at Christ Church, Doncaster, August 1975
XWU 890G was a Roe-bodied Leyland PDR1/1 that was new to T. Severn & Sons in 1969. The Albion badge was applied because the chassis was from a cancelled Scottish order. As a result, it was unique insomuch that it was the only Albion Atlantean to be supplied south of the border. The Hull body style by Roe was probably used to speed up its completion by adding another chassis to their order. It became 1154 in the South Yorkshire PTE fleet in March 1979, but by January 1981 had been withdrawn. It was scrapped soon afterwards.

Leyland PDR1A/1 GYG 712J Leaving Christ Church, Doncaster, October 1975
GYG 712J was the second of two Alexander-bodied Leyland Atlanteans that were new to
T. Severn & Sons in 1971. It is seen leaving Christ Church on a Hatfield, Thorne and Moorends
service. It appears to have sustained considerable panel damage to the offside; it was unusual to
see a Severn's vehicle with such damage still in service.

Leyland PDR1/2 GWX 553C at Christ Church, Doncaster, September 1976
GWX 553C was a Leyland Atlantean PDR1/2 with a Roe H76F body that was new to T. Severn &
Sons in 1965. It was the company's first full-fronted double-deck bus. In April 1979 it became
1155 in the fleet of South Yorkshire PTE and remained in service with them until the end of
1980, before going for scrapping in early 1981. It was to retain its original livery until the end.

A Line-up of Back Ends at Severn's Dunscroft Depot, April 1977
HUG 32N heads a line of double-deck buses inside Severn's Dunscroft Depot. The image shows the variety of body styles used by this operator and the clean, modern facilities provided to keep the fleet in first-class condition. This depot, located on Bootham Lane, became the centre for operations to the east of Doncaster by SYPTE, and this was to continue under South Yorkshire Transport Limited in 1986.

Bedford YRQ RWY 301L at Christ Church, Doncaster, April 1977
RWY 301L was a Duple-bodied Bedford YRQ that had been new to Severn's in August 1972. As well as regular excursion and private hire work, it was often used on the service to Skyehouse, which had become a daily service in 1976, rather than Saturdays-only. This improved service was thanks to the subsidy provided by South Yorkshire PTE and continued when the takeover of Severn's had been completed in 1979. The coach became 1094 in the SYPTE fleet and was withdrawn in 1981, after which it was operated by several small companies. Finally, in 1985, it was converted into a motor home.

Bedford YRQ OWX 769M at the Sandtoft Gathering, July 1977
OWX 769M was a Bedford YRQ with a Plaxton forty-five-seat body. It had been delivered new to T. Severn & Sons in late 1973 and was used for stage carriage, excursion and private hire work. The coach became 1095 in the South Yorkshire PTE fleet, remaining based at Dunscroft Depot. It was disposed of in July 1980 and passed to a dealer in Scotland, subsequently working for several operators, and was last noted as belonging to Robertson in Elgin as late as June 1992.

Leyland PD3/4 BWW 654B Departs from Christ Church, Doncaster, 28 August 1977
BWW 654B, a Roe-bodied Leyland PD3/4, had been delivered new to Severn's in August 1964 as their last new half-cab double-deck bus. After the South Yorkshire PTE takeover in March 1979, it remained in service for just over a year as fleet number 1156 before being withdrawn and converted into a recovery vehicle, numbered M18. It remained in the fleet and was transferred to South Yorkshire Transport Limited in October 1986. After its working life was over, it was purchased for preservation.

Leyland PD3/4 517 WY at Christ Church, Doncaster, September 1977
517 WY was a 1961 Roe-bodied Leyland PD3/4. It is seen on familiar duties in the last
days of service before withdrawal. Earlier photographs of it, seen on pages 76 and 79,
show that it remained very similar in appearance throughout its sixteen-year career.
The livery and advertisement were the same, for instance, with only the addition of
the Severn's garter logo in the 1960s.

Leyland AN68A/1R WYG 256S at Christ Church, Doncaster, July 1978
WYG 256S was the second of two Roe-bodied Leyland AN68A/1Rs delivered new to
Severn's in November 1977. It was the last double-deck bus acquired by the company
before the takeover by South Yorkshire PTE in March 1979. It became 1136 in their
fleet and was withdrawn and scrapped in 1986.

AEC Reliance PWX 591E on Private Hire Work, September 1978
PWX 591E was an AEC Reliance with a Plaxton Derwent body. It had been new to Severn's in June 1967 and became 1082 in the South Yorkshire PTE fleet after the takeover. After withdrawal from service in June 1983, it became the transport for a Sheffield marching band.

Leyland Atlantean XWU 890G at Christ Church, Doncaster, September 1978
T. Severn & Sons' XWU 890G was a Roe-bodied Leyland Atlantean PDR1/1 that had been delivered new to Severn's in January 1969. The bus was to retain its Severn's livery during its short working life as South Yorkshire PTE 1154.

Leyland Atlantean GYG 712J in Stainforth, November 1978
GYG 712J was the second of two 1971 Alexander-bodied Leyland Atlantean
PDR1A/1s. It is seen heading through Stainforth on the Dunscroft to Doncaster
service. Within six months the company and service would be taken over by South
Yorkshire PTE and the bus would be numbered 1153.

Bedford VAM14 OWW 435E at Severn's Dunscroft Depot, July 1979
OWW 435E was a Bedford VAM14 with a Plaxton body, and was delivered new
in March 1967 to Mosley of Barugh Green. It was bought by T. Severn & Sons in
February 1971 and became 1058 in the South Yorkshire PTE fleet. In June 1980 it
started a new life in the north-east of England, being operated by various organisations
and latterly by Stainton Grove District Council in May 1991. Its last manifestation
was as a traveller's home, after which it was scrapped.

Bedford YRQ OWX 769M at Severn's Dunscroft Depot, July 1979
OWX 769M was a Bedford YRQ with a Plaxton forty-five-seat body. It became 1095 in the South Yorkshire PTE fleet three months prior to this photograph being taken, receiving the barely visible fleet numbers on the front bodywork to the right of the headlight cluster. By July 1980 it had been sold and was at work in Scotland.

Leyland Atlantean HUG 33N at Christ Church, Doncaster, September 1979
HUG 33N was the second of two Roe-bodied Leyland AN6/1Rs delivered new to T. Severn & Sons in February 1985. It is seen after the takeover by South Yorkshire PTE and displays its new fleet number, 1138. It retained its original livery for a short time before it was repainted. It was to complete six years with the PTE before its withdrawal.

Leyland BWW 654B at the Reliance Garage in Stainforth, October 1979
Ex-Severn's Leyland PD3/4 BWW 654B had become South Yorkshire PTE 1156 in March 1979.
At the time Blue Line and Reliance had also been acquired by the PTE and they had lost two
double-deck buses in a road accident. BWW 654B was used as a replacement but had to be fitted
with makeshift destination blinds to suit the routes it would now be working. (Photograph J. B. Platt)

Leyland PD3/4 BWW 654B at the Winning Post Terminus, Moorends, October 1979
BWW 654B, a 1964 Roe-bodied Leyland PD3/4, was still looking quite presentable in 1979,
when photographed. It is seen wearing 1156 on its front, the fleet number it was given by its new
owners, South Yorkshire PTE, while standing at the Moorends Winning Post terminus of the
Thorne–Hatfield–Doncaster service. (Photograph J. B. Platt)

Leyland PD3/4 BWW 654B at Christ Church, Doncaster, April 1980
BWW 654B, a 1964 Roe-bodied Leyland PD3/4, had gained a certain celebrity status by the time this photograph had been taken and it was the last ex-independent half-cab double-deck bus still in passenger service. It would go on to be modified into a recovery vehicle and has now been preserved.

Leyland Atlantean SWR 4L at Christ Church, Doncaster, April 1980
SWR 4L, a Leyland AN68/1R with a Roe body, had been new to T. Severn & Sons in November 1972. After the takeover of the company by South Yorkshire PTE in March 1979, it became 1151 in their fleet. It was quickly repainted into the livery of its new owners and continued in service for another five years.

Leyland Atlantean XWU 890G at Christ Church, Doncaster, October 1980

XWU 890G was a Leyland Atlantean PDR1/1 with a Roe H75F body that was new in 1969 to T. Severn & Sons. In April 1979 it became 1154 in the fleet of South Yorkshire PTE but retained its green and cream livery and Albion badge until its withdrawal in August 1981.

A Line-up at Bootham Lane Depot, Dunscroft, August 1981

This line-up of ex-independent buses from left to right are: HWW 763/4J; GYG 711J; WYG 256S; HUG 33N; and JKY 264P. All five were based at the South Yorkshire PTE depot on Bootham Lane, Dunscroft, which had been inherited from T. Severn & Sons. These double-deck buses would all work for another three to five years before withdrawal, with WYG 256S eventually being preserved.

Leyland PD3/4 Recovery Vehicle 518 WY, June 1986
518 WY was a 1961 Roe-bodied Leyland PD3/4, which had been withdrawn by Severn's at the time of the takeover by South Yorkshire PTE in March 1979. It was converted for use as a recovery vehicle and became M17 in the SYPTE fleet. It was eventually transferred to the fleet of South Yorkshire Transport Limited in October 1986 and was scrapped in 1990.